HOW TO

ACCESSORIZE

HOW TO ACCESSORIZE

A Perfect Finish to Every Outfit

MICAELA ERLANGER

Illustrations by Babeth Lafon

CLARKSON POTTER/PUBLISHERS

NEW YORK

THIS BOOK IS DEDICATED
TO MY CLIENTS, *who are the ultimate*
and most inspiring muses. Thank you for
continually bringing fashion to life.

You can have anything you want in life, if you dress for it.

Styling is storytelling. As a stylist, when I create a red carpet look, I'm not simply choosing a dress, rather I'm creating a moment that becomes a part of history.

All my life, I have been styling. I was styling long before I knew it could even be a career. Some of my earliest memories are of playing dress-up, whether with my dolls, my little sister, or my high school girlfriends on a Friday night.

I carried my inherent love of fashion through my education at Parsons School of Design. During college, one of my first internships was at Condé Nast, where I had the opportunity to work in many different departments at various magazines. I found the experience thrilling. Come my senior year, I landed an internship at Hearst, in the fashion features department at one of their fashion publications. My boss let me go to photo shoots, where I would steam the clothes, dress the models, and pin everything to look perfect. It was very basic styling, but I loved it.

When I graduated from Parsons in 2008, I had the right degree at the wrong time. I wanted to be a fashion editor, but magazines were downsizing and no one was hiring, so I needed to become resourceful. Through a mutual connection, I heard that Annabel Tollman, a top celebrity stylist, was looking for an intern. I worked as her intern for a year, treating it like a job and learning everything I possibly could. Dressing celebrities in high fashion was exhilarating, hard work and completely different from the editorial world.

After a year, I began to get referrals for paid assistant jobs, and I landed a freelance gig working with a costume designer on a commercial. The job went well and she invited me to LA to work on a movie. Just like that, I bought a one-way ticket, packed up my inflatable mattress and my styling bag, and headed west.

My time in LA was straight out of a coming-of-age story. I slept on friends' couches and floors and drove a Rent-A-Wreck, which is a car on its way to the junkyard that you can rent for fifteen dollars a day. None of my car doors matched in color, and I was driving on spare tires. This was before GPS was ubiquitous, so I would print out my MapQuest directions and do my own navigating, all the while hoping my car wouldn't break down, which it did many, many times.

It may not have been the most glamorous time of my life, but I forged so many great connections. My nine months in Los

Angeles confirmed what I already knew: that fashion was where I wanted to be, and that I missed New York.

Back in NYC, I heard that Annabel was looking for a new assistant. I immediately called her, and lucky for me, she hired me back. I put my heart and soul into the job. I worked as her right hand for the next four years, and she became an incredible mentor.

Relationships are everything. One day, the lead makeup artist from a film I'd worked on reached out to me. We'd stayed in touch through the years, and thanks to her, I landed my first celebrity client, Michelle Dockery. After an incredible year working together, I felt ready to start my own company—even with only one client to my name. Some people doubted that a then-twenty-seven-year-old could succeed as a fashion stylist in a competitive and cutthroat industry, but I put their lack of confidence and my own fears aside in order to pursue my passion.

For the first year I was in business, I worked from home, surrounded by racks of clothes and shoes. I kept FedEx boxes in my bathtub while I showered at the gym and displayed trays of jewelry on my couch and handbags on my TV console. It was stressful and wonderful all at once, but it paid off.

About a year after starting my business, Michelle introduced me to her friend Lupita Nyong'o, and I began working with her. I dressed her for the awards season, culminating with the 2014 Academy Awards, where she won the Oscar for Best Actress in a Supporting Role in *12 Years a Slave* wearing a perfect pale-blue custom-designed Prada dress that made headlines around the world. Before I knew it, Hollywood was calling.

Just two years after starting my business, the *Hollywood Reporter* named me the third most powerful stylist in Hollywood. It was an incredible honor, and I am proud to say I've remained at the top of that list ever since.

When people talk about my work, one acknowledgment in which I take great pride is being credited with transforming clients from actors or musicians into fashion icons. In 2016, I was honored with an inaugural *Marie Claire* Image Makers award for my work with Lupita. People often associate her with wearing color, prints, or experimenting with edgy fashion, all of which is true. But one of the things she does so well is truly embrace accessories. Her Oscars headband had its own Twitter account! I've also been responsible for creating memorable uses of accessories, such as a lapel pin on Common, who has made the "man brooch," also known as a "jabot," his signature style.

There are so many different factors that go into creating a "best dressed" moment—the perfect dress, the hair and makeup, the accent jewelry. When the stars align, a look feels like an organic extension of the person wearing it. There's a certain feeling that arises when you're dressed in something that you really love. When it all comes together, people stop and take notice, because they feel the emotion and energy behind it.

That feeling is my favorite part of what I do. Whether I'm backstage at the Oscars, fluffing my client's train on the red carpet, or jetting around the world working on an ad campaign, I love that my job is to make people feel good. What could be more amazing than to know you're a part of some of the most memorable moments in someone's life? (Though as a fashion-obsessed person, getting to surround myself with beautiful things doesn't hurt, either.)

Whether it's on the street or the red carpet, the best fashion moments happen when someone's personality shines through. Getting dressed should be done with a sense of playfulness, whimsy, and joy. Whether you're dressing up for the most special day of your life, a Friday night date, a job interview, or just a trip to the supermarket, I want you to feel and look your absolute best. No matter where you are or what your personal style, I hope this book helps you create your own signature look.

I love helping my clients find that final touch that makes everything come together. It can come in many forms: a piece of jewelry, a red lip, a statement shoe. I always say it's like adding punctuation, where one small addition changes the whole message. That is the power of accessorizing.

In this book, we'll first cover the accessorizing basics, such as how to create a focal point or how to choose the right look for the occasion. Then, we'll talk about the types of accessories from head to toe and how to style each one. Accessories allow you to do so much with so little—they can even reinvent your entire wardrobe. It doesn't have to be scary or daunting. Sure, there are some dos and don'ts, but what follows is a simple guide. By the end, you'll be fully versed in the art of accessorizing. Now, let's get dressed!

PART

1

ACCES SORIES 101

An accessory is that extra touch you add to an outfit to make it yours. Whether shoes, bags, belts, or jewelry, accessories add dimension to your look, pull any outfit together, and instantly add polish. Every time you get dressed, it's a chance to express your personality, and accessories are the easiest way to do that. In my opinion, you can never have enough options in your closet! If the idea of accessorizing feels daunting, or if you're looking for some pointers, this is an easy guide to everything you need to know.

HOW TO CREATE A FOCAL POINT

14

There is an art to accessorizing, whether you are minimalist, maximalist, or somewhere in between. You don't need to wear everything you own, all at once, on one arm. Accessories have the most impact when there is a purpose behind them. The more thoughtful your choices, the more of a statement they will make.

Whenever you get dressed, decide which one area of your look you want to highlight. You may want to bring attention to a specific accessory (like an incredible statement necklace), accentuate a certain body part (like your legs), or highlight an aspect of your outfit (like an amazing print). The one you choose becomes your focal point for accessorizing.

For example, let's say you're wearing a dress with a plunging neckline. Do you choose to draw attention to that low neck by adding a necklace? Do you instead choose to highlight your face by wearing beautiful earrings, which will draw the eye upward? Or, do you choose to highlight your waist by adding a belt at the smallest point? Because you're being strategic, you would only choose one of these options, depending on your personal preference.

Yes, there is such a thing as being overaccessorized (unless you're the great Iris Apfel, who makes the look her own). You don't want to look like Miss Havisham or that lady who picked up every bauble on her way out of the department store. You know the one I'm talking about.

Coco Chanel once advised, "A lady should look in the mirror and remove one accessory before leaving the house." Yet some people swear by the philosophy "more is more." Since accessorizing is a personal statement, there is no single right answer. It's about understanding balance. When in doubt, remember to create a focal point. Go all out with the jewelry on your arms and wrists, or go all out decorating your face and neck, then go simple everywhere else.

THE RIGHT WAY TO GET DRESSED

There is no right order in which to get dressed. Everyone has his or her own formula. But there is logic to building a look. Whenever I put together an outfit, whether it's for a client or myself, I always ask a few questions to make sure the outfit is appropriate: *What is the occasion? Where am I going? What is the weather? What will I be doing? Do I want to make a statement?*

Once you've answered these questions, you can follow a few different recipes for putting together a look:

BASE YOUR OUTFIT AROUND AN ACCESSORY

Build an outfit around a specialty piece, be it a statement necklace or a bag that's encrusted with jewels. You are dressing up to be looked at. With this recipe, your chosen accessory is the focal point, and the rest of your outfit works around it and supports it.

INCORPORATE ACCESSORIES AS PUNCTUATION

Add accessories to pump up an otherwise everyday look. First, decide which message you want to communicate (professional, polished, sporty, and so forth) and choose your base outfit. Then, select an accessory that will make you stand out. For example, if you're wearing a basic silhouette or a relatively neutral palette, you might add a colorful bag or an unexpected shoe.

EVERYDAY ACCESSORIZING

With this recipe, your accessories blend more seamlessly into the rest of your look. If you're wearing a black sweater, you might pair it with a matching black bag and black shoes. If there is an area of your body you want to highlight, you might add a belt or wear high heels. Your accessories make your overall look cohesive, but they aren't the focal point.

*Reinvent Your Wardrobe Using
Three Accessorizing Tricks*

18

We all have those moments when we're sick of our clothes and want to revamp our entire wardrobe. Before you run out and buy a whole new closet, try these tricks to make what you own feel new.

1

SWAP OUT YOUR BAG

Switch your everyday bag for an updated version or a special bag you don't normally carry. Since a handbag is something you use daily, you'll get a lot of mileage out of it, and it will make your clothes feel fresh by association.

ADD A COLORFUL SHOE

Whether it's a solid or a print, adding a bright shoe is an easy way to make even the most basic outfit feel fun and surprising.

ADD STATEMENT JEWELRY

Try pairing unexpected jewelry with everyday attire, like big crystal earrings with your favorite T-shirt.

Always invest in your shoes and bags, because they will get you through the season and elevate the rest of your look. High-quality shoes and bags will last forever and give you a great bang for your buck. When it comes to jewelry, though, it doesn't always need to be real. Good costume jewelry (see page 66) can be a great way to dress up your wardrobe without breaking the bank.

365 DAYS OF DRESSING

THE RULES OF SEASONALITY

Do you ever find yourself wondering if it's appropriate to wear a certain piece from season to season? Some things are obvious (a wintry fur jacket, a beachy straw hat), while others are a bit trickier. Here are some simple guidelines:

	Cotton	Silk	Satin
ALWAYS APPROVED	X	X	X
RESERVE FOR SPRING/SUMMER			
RESERVE FOR FALL/WINTER			

Leather	Suede	Linen	Straw	Open weave	Washed silk	Velvet	Jacquard	Brocade	Thick knits	Heavy wools	Furs
X	X										
		X	X	X	X						
						X	X	X	X	X	X

You can always take a cue from colors. Lighter-colored accessories, especially pastels, are generally reserved for spring and summer. Jewel tones and darker shades are traditionally worn in winter months. Neutral colors and bright, classic hues may be worn all year round. At the end of the day, though, color is one area where you can play (such as a pastel winter coat or dark-colored sundress). These rules are not written in stone.

THE TRANSITION

HOW TO MOVE FROM DAY TO NIGHT

Sometimes you need your outfit to do double or triple duty, taking you from work to drinks to a dinner date. To transition any outfit from day to night, here are three simple steps:

DOWNSIZE

Swap out your everyday bag or work tote for something smaller in size, like a clutch.

GLITZ-IFY

Add something sparkly that's a bit bigger than your everyday jewelry, like a statement earring, cuff, or necklace.

GLAM YOUR GAMS

If you're wearing flats, trade them for high heels.

VOILÀ! THOSE THREE THINGS ARE ALL YOU NEED.

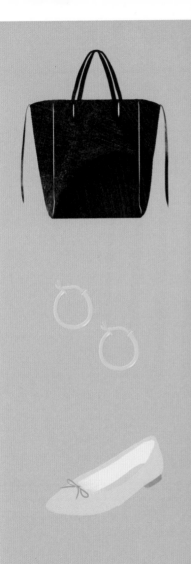

DAY

NIGHT

2

FROM
HEAD
TO
TOE

HATS
AND HAIR
ACCESSORIES

Hats are outerwear and can be used for practical purposes, such as for warmth, to shade you from the sun, or to hide a bad hair day. But they can also add style and elevate your look. Sometimes, a hat may be part of a tradition or dress code for formal occasions. However you wear a hat, it should always be with a personal touch.

Hair accessories are like jewelry for your head. Whether it's a headband or comb, adding a hair accessory is an easy way to give your outfit a little extra something and look as if you've put thought into your appearance. When done correctly, it can lend a subtle touch—or have maximum impact.

HATS

The hat is an underrated accessory. Hats are sometimes the perfect complement to an outfit— although wearing them requires advanced accessorizing skills.

When choosing a hat, it's important to understand hat-to-head proportion. You want a hat that fits both your head and your face shape. It should sit nicely on your head and not look too big! Your hat should also fit the mood and overall vibe of your look.

Note

Even if your hair just isn't cooperating one day, good manners would have you remove your hat when you're indoors (and to be honest, I agree).

1   A **wide brim hat**, such as a **fedora** or **trilby**, is one of the easiest to wear, as it doesn't discriminate when it comes to face shape or head size. Look for felt, wool, or suede in dark, neutral shades, such as brown, navy, camel, or burgundy.

---

2   **Berets** should be worn to the side. Avoid making your look too literal by pairing a beret with anything overtly Parisian, like a black turtleneck or striped shirt. Berets look great with menswear-inspired suiting or a belted coat.

---

3   During the winter months, **beanies** are good for warmth and are especially fun with a pom-pom or in a bright color. Fall and winter are the only times when wearing a knit hat is appropriate.

---

4   I love **straw hats**, either on the beach or paired with a sundress. They offer both sun protection and style.

5   A **fisherman's cap** looks great with an overcoat and can also be worn with a T-shirt or jean jacket in fall or spring. It is *not* the same as a newsboy cap, which has a shorter brim and, in my opinion, should be avoided.

---

6   **Baseball caps** are awesome weekend wear and will make any outfit more casual. These days, you can easily find one without any insignias or logos. Go for traditional materials, like cotton canvas.

---

7   A **fascinator** is a style of headpiece traditionally worn in place of a hat. They are often adorned with embellishments such as feather, flowers, or beads. Fascinators are appropriate for very specific occasions, including weddings, horse races, or formal evening events. They are generally reserved for royalty or aristocracy, or the likes of Carrie Bradshaw.

Hang your hats on a hook or keep them in boxes. You can stack hats inside one another in a hatbox, which saves space and helps them retain their shape.

Stuffing plain, unscented tissue paper inside also preserves the right shape (such as with the little dip in the top of a fedora).

A tip for reviving any misshapen hat, especially straw or thin felt: Steam the hat from the underside to help it regain its shape. You can also use a low-heat iron with a pressing cloth to smooth out any bends.

When is it appropriate to wear a tiara?

The short answer: a tiara is only appropriate if you are royalty. The longer answer is a tiara is only occasionally appropriate and never truly necessary. Tiaras should be worn only to costume parties or the most formal of events, such as white-tie events and state occasions. They should be worn for evening affairs only (again, unless you are actually a princess).

HAIR ACCESSORIES

I adore a **headband**. It's minimal effort and can have major impact on your look. On the practical side, it's also a great way to hold your hair back. There are daytime headbands, evening headbands, and bejeweled or embellished headbands.

For daytime, good options are tortoiseshell, enamel, and fabric. If you don't have a headband, you can achieve the same effect by tying a black grosgrain ribbon or silk scarf around your head and knotting it at the nape of your neck.

If you're going for an embellished headband, make sure to keep your outfit and above-the-neck jewelry simple, since there's a lot going on near your face. For example, a headband should be worn in lieu of big earrings, so it's best to forgo them or stick with small studs.

Barrettes and pretty **hair combs** add an element of surprise, especially when worn on the back of the head. They can be either embellished or plain. As with all accessories, if you're opting for a barrette, this becomes your focal point. So keep the rest of the area minimal—that is, don't wear a barrette, a scarf, *and* hoop earrings. For embellished versions, I recommend looking for the clearest crystals, and I prefer floral or modern geometric designs. For plain barrettes, look for options made of plain black lacquer, wire or metal, enamel, or tortoiseshell, which will help keep the look sophisticated and age appropriate.

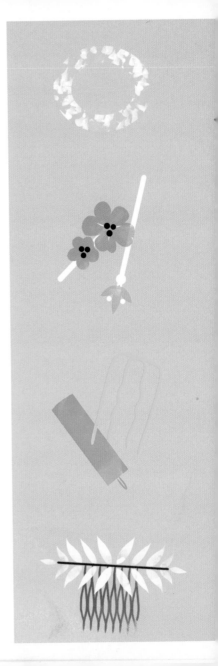

SUNGLASSES

Before you head outside, think of sunglasses almost like a piece of jewelry you wear on your face.

I recommend owning three pairs: one black, one tortoiseshell, and one sporty. The most important part of choosing a pair is to understand your face shape. If you don't know your face shape, take a good look in the mirror and compare it to the illustrations that follow. If you still have trouble making a determination, try looking in a mirror and tracing the outline of your face with your finger or a washable dry-erase marker.

SQUARE

You have strong, well-defined angles along your forehead, cheeks, and jaw. Square faces are flattered by frames with soft, round shapes, including cat-eye, round, and aviator styles.

HEART

Your face is characterized by a broad forehead that tapers down to a narrower jawline. Heart-shaped faces look good in sunglasses with thin frames, like aviators. A good trick is for the frames to be wider than your forehead.

OVAL

You have a long, relatively balanced face shape, with a jawline slightly narrower than your forehead. Lucky ovals can wear nearly any style frame.

ROUND

Your face is relatively circular, and about the same width and height.
Round faces look best in contrasting, angular frames, like rectangles and
squares, as well as some oversized looks.

Now that you understand your face shape, consider the period references behind each style. Here are the most common ones to know:

1 **Aviators**, originally designed for pilots in the 1930s, are a casual style with a distinctive teardrop shape. Often crafted with a wire frame, aviators give off a cool, sporty, and stylish vibe all at once.

---

2 **Cat-eye frames** have a glamorous 1950s-inspired shape that sweeps up in the outer corners, like the iconic frames Audrey Hepburn wore in *Breakfast at Tiffany's*. The silhouette makes them a bit more formal—a good choice for dressing up.

---

3 **Square** and **rectangular** styles—such as the popular Ray-Ban **Wayfarer**—tend to have a sporty feel. This style harks back to the '50s and '60s, when glasses shapes were modeled after Eames chairs and Cadillac fins. The Wayfarer surged back into popularity in the '80s, thanks to Tom Cruise in *Risky Business*. Rectangular styles are a good choice for everyday, particularly in black or tortoiseshell. Remember, the larger the frame, the more dramatic the effect.

---

4 **Round glasses** were trendy in the '80s and '90s, though their roots have a decidedly '60s vibe (think John and Yoko). You can dress them up or down.

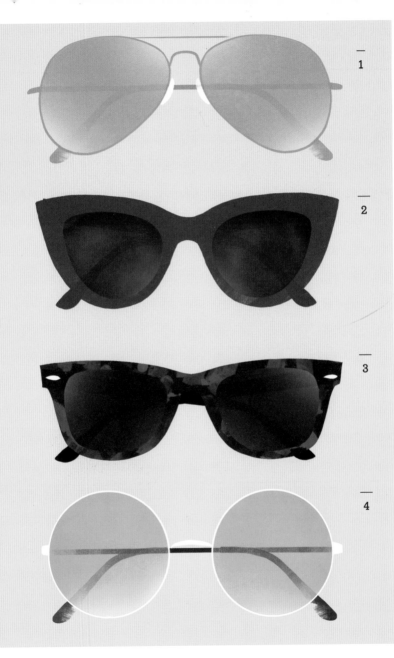

1

2

3

4

When choosing your sunglasses, consider the occasion, just as you would when choosing your shoes or bag. Will you be sitting poolside at a fancy hotel? Going to a baseball game? Attending an outdoor wedding? Or running around town doing errands?

For everyday wear, I always keep my go-to sunglasses in my work tote. Usually, I wear a pair of no-brainer black frames. Sometimes I'll swap them out for tortoiseshell glasses, which have a brown frame.

A formal occasion, like an outdoor wedding, is a good opportunity to wear more feminine, traditional shapes, or to play with colored lenses. As long as the sunglasses complement your overall look, you're okay.

The rules for choosing your lens and frame colors are the same as matching any other accessory: Pick something that complements the color scheme of the rest of your outfit. But remember, sunglasses are outerwear. Since you take them off whenever you are indoors, you don't need to worry about how they coordinate with your other above-the-neck accessories, unless your sunglasses are a major statement piece.

Finally, I like to avoid sunglasses with excess hardware. You'll get the most out of your investment if you choose a style without a lot of detailing.

I store my sunglasses in a drawer. To prevent scratches, always keep sunglasses in their case, along with a chamois cloth for easy cleaning.

If you have room to store your sunglasses out in the open, acrylic nail polish display cases are a great way to keep them organized.

Note on Special Lenses

Colored lenses—particularly yellow, pale blue, and rose—are a more contemporary look, though they can be tricky to wear. Look for versions with a wire frame and a light and delicate feel. When styling colored lenses, use the glasses as an accent to help play up the color in your outfit. **Polarized lenses**—reflective lenses that look like mirrors—are appropriate for any season, though they are best suited for sporty outfits and events.

JEWELRY

Jewelry is like the icing on a cake. It's what pulls a look together in its entirety.

When choosing jewelry, first consider the vibe you're going for. Is it bohemian? Glamorous? Contemporary? Classic? If your clothes are the main attraction, go simple with the jewelry. If you're wearing a simple outfit, you can afford to make more of a statement.

Next, consider tone. Does your outfit contain warmer hues, like peach, yellow, or red? Then stick with warm-toned jewelry, such as yellow and rose gold. For outfits with cooler tones, like blues, purples, and greens, accessorize with silver and gunmetal.

Mixing jewelry in different ways is what makes a look your own. Don't be afraid to combine your heirloom pieces with things that are newer, or to wear costume jewelry alongside the real thing, or to layer, stack, and group items together.

EARRINGS

1   **Stud earrings** are truly low-maintenance; you can even sleep in them. They are super versatile, especially if you don't want to change your earrings all the time. Diamonds, pearls, gemstones, or metal balls are some common examples and are all great options for everyday wear. If you have a go-to pair of earrings, your ears will never be bare.

---

2   **Chandelier earrings** are the most attention-grabbing style. If you're going there, it's best to pass on all the other bits and bobs. You can wear a statement earring with anything, from jeans to a party dress. I love styling chandelier earrings in unexpected ways, like with a vintage T-shirt or sweatshirt.

3   **Drop earrings** are a good middle ground between the stud and the chandelier. The drop earring has a base like an on-the-ear stud, with a dangly component. They're very versatile and look good with everything.

---

4   **Hoop earrings** are a classic silhouette that can work for both everyday and evening. They can feel playful or sexy, depending on the size and weight. Thinner is usually better. Choose a hoop that feels proportional to your face and the height of your neckline.

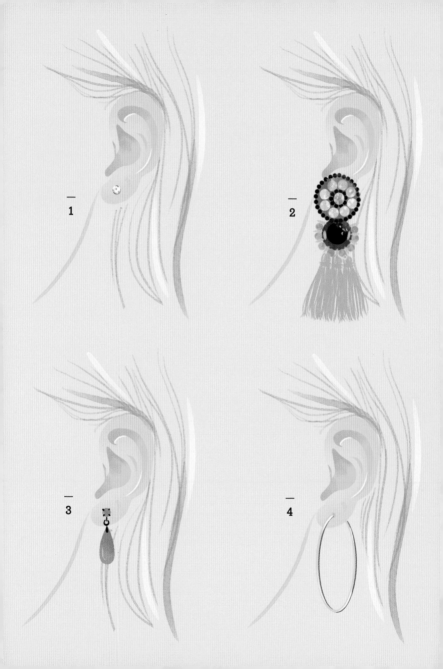

5   **Ear cuffs and crawlers** are an easy way to add edge or extra
    sparkle to your look. Ear cuffs typically slip around the cartilage,
    while crawlers climb up your lobe. These styles are a good way
    to experiment with an edgier look without having to commit to
    something permanent. The most important thing is finding a
    style that fits your ear properly. There are short versions, long
    versions, ones meant to go over cartilage, and others that fit into
    pierced ears. Wear them either asymmetrically, or as a pair—
    it's a personal choice!

Can you wear earrings and a necklace together?

You can get away with wearing studs and a necklace, but otherwise, you
should probably choose one or the other. Pairing chandelier earrings with
a statement necklace is a definite no, as they'll compete with each other
and overwhelm your face—and your outfit.

RINGS

1 **Cocktail rings** are a great way to add a statement, especially if you're trying to ease your way into jewelry. The more massive the ring, of course, the more of a showstopper it will be. Cocktail rings are typically worn on your index or middle finger, or on the ring finger of your right hand. But do note if you are wearing a cocktail ring, it doesn't necessarily need to be your only ring.

2 **Signet rings** are engraved with your personal monogram (usually one or three initials). These have been worn since the Middle Ages, when they were considered a status symbol. You can wear a signet ring on any finger, but it looks especially chic on your pinkie.

3 An **eternity ring** is a band with stones set all the way around that is generally worn as a wedding band. If you have one that is not a wedding band, you can stack it with other bands.

4 A **multi-finger ring** goes across two or more fingers and is a statement all by itself. If it's a statement you decide to make, you may want to forgo other jewelry in the hand and wrist area.

5 **Thumb rings**, traditionally in the form of a relatively unadorned band, have a very '90s feel.

IF THE RING FITS . . .

Size Your Rings

Your rings should fit snugly on your hand but not feel too tight. There should be some resistance when sliding the ring over your knuckle, and it shouldn't come loose, even when you wash your hands. A jeweler can help you determine the right size. Beware, though: Your size can change with the seasons, as fingers swell in warmer months.

PUT A RING ON IT / *Ring Styling Tips*

You can pair big rings with big earrings, since they're far from each other, but if choosing to make a statement on your fingers, seek balance. Try placing emphasis on alternate sides of the body, such as a statement ring on one hand and a statement bracelet on the other.

When wearing multiple rings, I like to wear them on every other finger to keep a bit of space in between. Stacking is an easy way to experiment with layering. I like to stack an odd number, usually three. Try a variety of widths, weights, and metals. Of course, make sure your hand feels comfortable and all rings are secure on your finger.

NECKLACES

Perhaps more than any other piece of jewelry,
a necklace has the power to anchor a look.

1   The above is especially true in the case of a **statement necklace.** A statement necklace is usually a wide, heavy, or bold necklace and can be of any silhouette. It could be adorned with colorful stones, sparkly crystals, or cool architectural details. A statement necklace will instantly add punch to a monochromatic look, but you can wear one with just about everything. I like pairing a statement necklace with a T-shirt to create that juxtaposition between fancy and casual and make something plain really pop.

As with any other statement piece, this necklace becomes the focal point and should be worn with minimal jewelry.

2   A **pendant necklace** features one main element that is suspended from a chain or cord. It's a super-broad definition and could be something everyday (a charm with your first initial) or elegant (a precious stone). Pendant necklaces come in every length imaginable— try them on and experiment to see what looks and feels best for you (see box on page 56).

3 A **rivière** necklace features a single strand of gemstones (typically diamonds) of the same size and cut. It should sit right on the collarbone.

4 A **choker** is a short necklace that wraps around the middle of the neck. It can be made of leather, fabric, or metal, and has a distinct '90s feel. But beware: If you have a short neck, this style is best avoided, as it cuts across and can make it appear even shorter.

5 A **collar** necklace is one that falls near the base of your neck, just below your collarbone. It is typically around 16" long.

Go to Great Lengths

There are some technical terms to define specific lengths of necklaces.

At 18" in length, a **princess** necklace falls on the upper chest.

The **matinee** necklace is typically 22–24" long, falling near the décolleté.

A 30" **opera-length necklace** falls close to the waist. As the name suggests, necklaces of this length are typically reserved for more formal looks.

OFF THE CHAIN
Necklace Styling Tips

An open neckline (with lots of skin showing) lets you highlight your necklace, as does a simple top or plain T-shirt.

A plunging neckline looks great with an opera necklace or even a layered, multi-strand look.

A collared shirt, unbuttoned at the neck, complements a collar or princess necklace, or a simple pendant that rests against your skin.

A simple crew-neck or off-the-shoulder top works nicely when paired with a collar-length necklace.

For events, you could even try a necklace worn in the hair, either as a headband or wrapped around the base of your ponytail.

Layering necklaces is about varying lengths so no two necklaces are competing. You also want to keep a bit of space between them. Try one short, one medium, and one super long. Stop after a few strands so you don't look weighed down!

Untangle Necklaces

When necklace chains become tangled, the knot can seem utterly impossible to undo. But here's the secret:

Take two needles or safety pins.

Gently but firmly place one pin into the center of the knot.

Holding the first pin stationary, use the second pin to delicately pull and coax the knot apart.

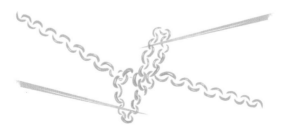

It might take a few minutes, but eventually it will work.

BRACELETS AND WATCHES

Bracelets and watches are easy to incorporate into your everyday wear. They offer a lot of flexibility; you can dress your outfit up by adding a bracelet, or you can dress your bracelets down by adding a watch. On a practical note, make sure your wristwear doesn't compete with your sleeves and that they sit properly on your wrist and don't hang too low.

1 A **cuff** is a relatively wide metal or enamel bracelet with a split in the band that allows it to slide directly onto your wrist. One wide cuff makes a standalone statement. Two matching cuffs, one on either wrist, make quite the impression.

2 A **bangle** is a solid, circular bracelet, often slipped over your hand. Bangles come in many materials, including metal, enamel, Lucite, Bakelite (a rare, beautiful resin from the 1920s and '30s), and wood. Multiple bangles jingle and jangle, so keep that in mind! They're not the best choice if you're going to be typing on a keyboard all day, or if you're headed to a quiet event or performance where noise is not appreciated.

3 **Chain bracelets** are made with flexible metal links, making them easy to have resized, and they often close with a clasp. They can be ID bracelets or just plain links. A chunkier version with pendants attached is a charm bracelet.

---

4 **Tennis bracelets** have stones, typically diamonds, set all the way around. They are thin and flexible and secured with a clasp.

5 **Watches** are practical items, but they are also a piece of jewelry. When it comes to fit, a good rule of thumb is to make sure the base sits next to your wrist bone. Oversized watches have a casual feel, while daintier watches are more formal.

Group bracelets in odd numbers—typically three or five. Unless your bracelets are super thin, seven is probably too many. Hard, structured pieces like bangles stack better than flexible bracelets with links. The most important thing is creating a stack that sits nicely together. Try bracelets with different thicknesses and weights. You can also try **layering a watch** with bracelets. Add the watch first and then layer on a couple bracelets of differing weights.

BROOCHES

Not just for your grandma, brooches are fun to play with and are great for layering on jackets, sweaters, and even your handbag. Try them in unexpected places, such as the tips of your collar, and with unexpected clothing, such as more masculine pieces. You can even attach them to a comb and wear them in your hair.

For more punch, try grouping brooches together in odd numbers, and don't be afraid to layer up! I love to cluster big brooches mixed with little pins of varying sizes.

FAKE IT TILL YOU MAKE IT
Elevate Your Look with Costume Jewelry

Jewelry is an area where it's okay to experiment with a range of styles and prices. There is so much variety in the world of costume jewelry and a lot of opportunity to have fun. Generally, when shopping for costume jewelry, you want to pick things that look expensive, even if they're not.

Keep an eye out for enamels, gold plating, and brass items that won't tarnish or lose their color. Crystals should be clear and ultra-sparkly. Colored stones should look realistic in terms of color and size. Avoid cloudy stones, anything that's discolored or chipped, and beware of anything that rubs off on your hands. Also pass on obvious knockoffs. Last but not least, go for quality: the heavier the metal, the better!

Mix Metals

You can mix metals in your jewelry. Personally, I prefer to keep everything in the same family, which means either mixing warmer metallic shades, like yellow with rose gold, or cooler metallic shades, like silver with gunmetal. However, you can also mix warm and cool tones as long as you keep it balanced.

Try mixing pieces in odd numbers, like wearing three bracelets where two are yellow gold and one is rose. It's also important to carry the mixed theme throughout your entire look. Consider the tones of all your jewelry, as well as the tones of any hardware on your handbag and belt, to create a mix that feels balanced and intentional.

A **jewelry box** is a magical thing. Whether it has drawers or interior compartments, or is even a whole chest, a jewelry box will keep everything organized, prevent tangles, and prevent tarnishing.

If you don't have a jewelry box, you can also try a **jewelry tree**, which has hooks to keep everything from getting tangled.

Rings, studs, and other small items look pretty displayed in little **dishes** or **trays**, which also keep your everyday accessories easily accessible.

Plain old **hooks** are also a great option for visually displaying necklaces and keeping them untangled. You can find inexpensive options at your local hardware or craft store.

A **mesh screen** is another great idea for storing and displaying earrings.

When packing your jewelry for travel, it's important to place everything in separate pouches, made of velvet or silk, to prevent scratches, knots, and wear and tear. In a pinch, you can also separate pieces into small plastic bags.

SCARVES

Scarves can either be worn for practical reasons (warmth) or can be used as a layering tool to add another element to your look.

When wearing a scarf for warmth, there are a few easy ways to style it. You can fold it in half, then pull the two ends through the loop. You can wrap the scarf one time around your neck, so the ends of the scarf are a little uneven. Or, you can wrap the scarf around your neck a couple times, then tuck the ends in, to make a continuous loop.

A **shawl** is an oversized scarf that can be draped around your shoulders.

A **pashmina** is generally made of either cashmere or a silk blend. They are thinner than scarves and shawls and are usually wrapped around the shoulders to provide warmth for evening (or in the event of over–air conditioning). If you want to wear a pashmina for everyday, you can style it as you would a scarf.

A **silk scarf**, usually worn purely as an accessory (rather than for warmth), can be styled in many ways. Here are three of my favorites:

AROUND THE NECK,
AS A CHOKER

Fold the opposite corners
of your scarf inward,
toward the center.

Continue folding alternate
sides until you are left with
a long, thin strand.
(figs. 1 & 2)

Tie the two ends
together, so the scarf sits
just against your neck.
Depending on the length
of your scarf, you may
wish to double knot it.
(fig. 3)

For more of a choker effect,
turn the scarf so the tails
are in the back.

1

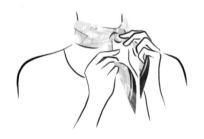

2

3

Note

This looks especially chic paired
with a crisp collared shirt.

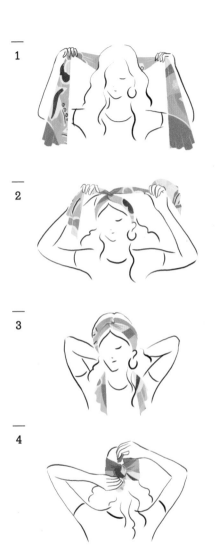

1

2

3

4

Begin with a long rectangular scarf or a large square folded in half to create a rectangle.

Line up the center of the scarf with the back of your head. *(fig. 1)*

Take one end of the scarf in either hand and cross them over each other in front of your face, creating a little twist. *(fig. 2)*

Wrap the ends toward the back of your head. *(fig. 3)*

Tie them in a knot at the base of your neck. Depending on the length of your scarf, either tuck the loose ends into the base of the scarf or wrap and tuck them along the sides. *(fig. 4)*

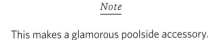

Note

This makes a glamorous poolside accessory.

WORN TRADITIONALLY AS A BANDANA

Fold your scarf diagonally in half. *(fig. 1)*

Take the opposite side of the scarf and fold it toward the center. Continue this under you've reached your desired width. *(fig. 2)*

Tie the bandana loosely around your neck. *(fig. 3)*

Note

For an easy way to elevate an outfit, try a silk scarf tied around the handle of your handbag.

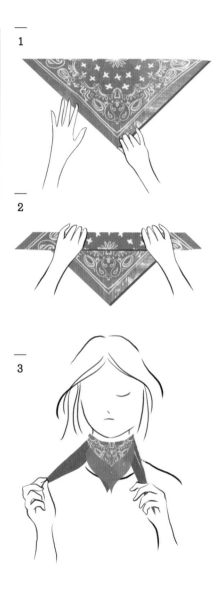

GET ORGANIZED / *Scarf Storage Tips*

I keep my scarves neatly folded in a box in my closet. You can also keep them folded in a drawer, using drawer dividers.

Scarves can also be draped across the bottom of a hanger. Otherwise, I advise against hanging them, as they are too delicate and can become damaged easily.

BELTS

First things first: Belts should not be worn to hold up your pants.

If your pants cannot stay up on their own, they don't fit. When used properly, however, belts can define your waist, accent your look, or do both.

Belts, to me, are almost like a piece of jewelry. It's important to understand and consider the hardware of the belt. A buckle can be very distracting and must coordinate with the rest of your outfit, the same way you would treat mixing metals in jewelry (see page 67).

Belts come in every material imaginable: leather, patent, metal, fabric, pony hair, and exotic skins. I recommend having one black, one brown, one metal, and one wide style.

Belts can either be worn low (slung around the hips) or high (at the actual smallest point of your waist). For most people, the narrowest part of the body is where your belly button is. When you wear a belt at the smallest point, it really draws the eye inward, helping to define your waist and give you more shape.

It's important to consider the width of the belt in proportion to the rest of your outfit. If you're wearing a very narrow, slender silhouette, such as a form-fitting dress, you can afford to wear a bigger belt. If you're wearing an outfit with more volume on the bottom, like a wide-leg pant, then you want to draw the eye inward at the waist. Opt for a thinner belt to balance out the look.

Like any accessory, you want your belts to be neat and visually accessible. If you have room in your closet, hang them from a belt rack (a tie rack works fine, too).

Another option is to coil your belts and store them in a shallow drawer organized by dividers, or in a shoe box.

Does your belt need to match your shoes?

Your shoes and belt should always be complementary. The foolproof trick is to match them exactly (for example, wearing both shoes and a belt made of black leather). Or you can pull out a color, material, or finish that you want to highlight (for example, pairing a navy belt with patterned shoes that have navy blue accents). If you're experimenting with color blocking, a belt is also a good place to do that.

1 Try wearing a belt over your sweater, over a blazer, even over your coat. I love belting a turtleneck sweater dress to give myself some shape!

2 You don't always have to fasten a belt in the traditional way; you can also knot it! If you want a cleaner look, try turning the belt around, so the buckle is in the back.

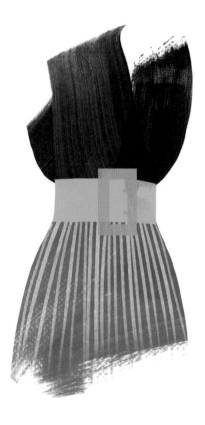

3 You can even belt more body-con outfits with a very wide belt, which will act almost like a corset. You can also use this trick if you feel conscious of your tummy. The more you understand your unique shape and what works best on your body, the more experimental you can get.

HOSIERY
AND LINGERIE

Wearing hosiery—socks, stockings, and tights—as an accessory can be a challenge. When you choose to make it an accessory, it means you aren't wearing it for its basic purpose (warmth or comfort), but because you intend for it to be seen.

SOCKS

Unless I am wearing socks for warmth, I usually vote to skip them. But a sock becomes an accessory when you choose to wear it with heels, with sandals, or as a novelty sock with flat, lace-up shoes.

Accessorizing with socks is advanced. If you're going there, it's important to choose a thin material. It can be opaque or sheer, patterned, or in a silk blend. For the most flattering effect, choose socks that end at the smallest part of your leg, typically three or four inches above your anklebone.

Socks worn as accessories become a focal point, so you don't want them to detract from the rest of your outfit. For maximum impact, choose a sock in a color, whether it's an accent color or a complementary color that ties back to the rest of your outfit.

An over-the-knee sock looks especially cute paired with flat oxford shoes. I've also seen people wear over-the-knee socks peeking out from the top of a knee-high boot. As always, proportion is key. Play around until it feels like the sock hits at just the right spot. You want them to be visible, but subtle.

TIGHTS

Tights should be worn only in fall and winter months. Both sheer and opaque tights are meant for wear with dresses and skirts for warmth. Though it may seem obvious, it is also worth mentioning: You should *never* wear tights with holes in them!

Black tights go with everything. Opaque black tights are the most foolproof, but sheer black tights can be a good option, too. Since the skin peeks through a little bit, the color isn't as intense, and the look is a little sexier.

Colored, textured, and **patterned** tights can be a bit trickier. A simple repeating pattern, like a Swiss dot, is the easiest to pull off. When it comes to colored tights, my advice is to go dark or rich. Muted and jewel tones look the most flattering, and primary colors are best avoided. When wearing textured or patterned tights, they become the focal point, so avoid wearing pattern in the rest of your outfit.

Fishnets are truly advanced accessorizing. The rule of thumb here is that the less stocking showing, the better. I've seen some very fashionable women wear them in unexpected ways with amazing results. Think: a tiny peek of fishnet seen through ripped jeans. I've also seen little fishnet socks look cute. Never do you want to display a wide swath of fishnets. Fishnets come in nude and black, and occasionally colors, but my advice is to avoid wearing nude, unless you're performing. Stockings with the seam up the back are a very sexy, very boudoir look. As such, they are best kept in the bedroom.

BRAS AND SHAPEWEAR

Lingerie is to be worn under your clothes.
Wear things that fit comfortably, that don't pinch,
and that are seamless or otherwise undetectable
under your garments. Daring fashionistas
sometimes practice wearing lingerie as an
accessory. This might mean a colored bra under
a sheer top, or a bralette worn over a T-shirt.
Sometimes it can look nice to have a little hint
of lace peeking out in a way that isn't too overt.
But otherwise, I wouldn't advise anyone to wear
lingerie as outerwear. It isn't necessarily wrong,
but it is very tricky to get right! This is one look
best reserved for full-fledged fashionistas, just as
tiaras are reserved for royalty (see page 32).

When it comes to **bras**, fit is everything. Most women don't wear the right bra size, and your size changes over the years, so it's worth going to get measured. A bra should fit snugly—but not pinch—around the rib cage. The cup should fit your breast, meaning no spillage and no double boob. Also, the right size bra should fit comfortably when secured on the middle hook. The whole point of having multiple bra hooks is that as the elastic wears and the fit becomes looser, you can move to the smaller hole. Bras come in many styles and cuts, so I encourage you to try a bunch on to find what works best for your body.

Shapewear is your best friend. Good shapewear does exactly what it says, which is give you shape under your garments. It's smoothing and slimming and comes in a variety of high-tech fabrics. The most traditional forms are high-waisted shaping shorts, control pantyhose or underwear, contouring slips (also known as full-body shapers), and corsets.

The only time it is ever appropriate for shapewear to be seen is when it's layered, such as a shaping camisole with a lace detail worn under a blazer. Otherwise, your shapewear should match your skin tone and disappear under your clothes.

Socks and hosiery should be gently folded or rolled (never balled up or tied) and stored in drawers for easy access. I like to fold my bras in half (stacking cup into cup) and tuck the straps in, to help them hold their shape. Shapewear should be folded.

Lingerie is delicate and must be treated with care. Store it on its own, where it won't be pulled or crushed by heavier clothing. I like to use drawer organizers specifically designed for lingerie. If you have a favorite scent, add a sachet, scented papers, or even fancy soap (still in its wrapper).

93

Lingerie should be hand washed and air dried. Because the materials are delicate, find and use a soap or detergent specifically for your intimates. It will help to keep their elasticity and shape.

BAGS

*Bags are a necessity.
Once you have the basics,
fill out your wardrobe
with whatever you'd like—*

novelty bags, crazy colors, a totally
impractical bejeweled thing you carry
once every three years. But, for now,
let's talk about the basics.

1   A **top handle tote** is generally a frame-shaped bag with a handle that you carry in your hand or the crook of your arm. It often has a few compartments and has a very ladylike feel. The iconic example of this is the Hermès Birkin bag.

2   The **cross body** has a strap that goes across your body, making it ideal for everyday use, especially when you want your hands to remain free. They come in lots of different shapes and materials but are generally smaller in size.

3   An **evening bag** is a smaller, delicate bag that fits under your arm or in your hand. Evening bags come in all sorts of shapes and materials, including fabric, velvet, metal, skins, leather, and embellished crystal, though they are most often a little box or a minaudière. It's the bag equivalent of wearing a piece of fine jewelry. It doesn't fit much—just your keys, your powder or lipstick, and that's about it. You're lucky if it fits your cell phone!

4   A **day clutch** is a larger version of the evening bag. The size lends itself to feeling more casual, depending on the material and the shape. They are often envelopes or pouches. A clutch can be a statement item and is a great chance to have a lot of fun.

5   The **hobo** is a slouchy bag with a loose bucket shape, worn over the shoulder by a single strap. Often made of leather, hobos are typically large enough to hold your everyday essentials and are a casual, daytime style. It's not necessarily the most modern shape of bag.

6 The **carryall** or **work tote** is an oversized tote that does double duty, holding all of your everyday necessities, as well as any extras you may need to take you through the day, such as your wallet, laptop, notebook, and cosmetic case. It typically has a two-shoulder strap. The carryall is not to be confused with a **gym bag**, which is a washable fabric bag made especially for workout clothes and paraphernalia. It can also work well for the airport or as an overnight bag.

Ideally, you want one of each style, in brown and black leather. Your basic everyday bag should be made of leather or suede. You want the most durable materials, because the whole point of a bag is to carry your stuff (and stuff can be heavy). Look for little feet at the bottom, especially on larger bags such as work totes. They not only offer structure and support but also protect your bag from wear and tear.

For evening bags, it's ideal to have one black and one metallic. Your basic evening bags may be made of satin or a novelty material like metal. They can have embellishment of any kind.

The biggest tip I can offer is to choose bags with minimal hardware. You'll get the most longevity out of a bag without a lot of bells and whistles. The more understated and simple it is, the more timeless and versatile it will be. Bags are an investment, and you want them to last for as long as possible. For this same reason, I also look for bags without logos.

Luggage is an important category of its own. Your luggage—including both your carry-on bag and whatever baggage you're going to check—should be a neutral color. It's going to get dirty, so I look for colors and materials that will hold up against wear and tear. Go for ergonomics. Luggage that sits on four wheels is the easiest to handle. I prefer things that are lightweight and roomy—you have a lot of accessories to pack! But it's okay to keep style in mind. Hard cases are attractive and serve the purpose of protecting your stuff.

Your luggage is a fun thing to personalize. You might add a monogram or put stickers on it. A luggage tag is also a great accessory. If you like, you can even match your luggage, tag, and passport case to keep everything cohesive.

Most **leather** bags can be used year-round, especially if they are a neutral color.

If a bag has any kind of **straw** detailing, like a wicker or bamboo handle, reserve it for summer.

Skins are very specific and are not an everyday item. The longest lasting skins are python, water snake, and alligator. Ostrich and different kinds of lizard skin are popular choices, as well. Skins are a high-maintenance item and must be carried with care. You also need to store and protect them so the scales don't flake.

Pony hair is a novelty fabric, but it's pretty versatile. It has a nice luster and sheen to it and gives outfits a nice detail.

The downside of pony hair is that once it rubs off, it cannot be replaced. Once it's gone, it's gone. So it's best to reserve carrying it for special occasions.

EXTRAS

Bag accessories have become a trend, including pom-poms, tassels, and fun charms. They can be an easy way to inject a little personality and attitude into your look.

Monogramming—adding one's initials to leather goods—has been around since ancient Greece and is just about the preppiest thing one can do. But it is very chic, especially on totes and luggage.

GET ORGANIZED / *Bag Storage Tips*

Bags should be stored in their dust bags. I recommend keeping the dust bag pushed low enough so that you can see the handle or the top of the bag peeking out, which helps you easily find what you have in your closet.

To help retain their shape during storage, bags should be stuffed with plain, unscented tissue paper. *Do not* use newspaper, as the ink will smear.

In my closet, I like to organize by type (all evening bags together, all totes together, and so forth) and then within each category by color.

Sun damage is real, so always keep bags in a cool, dark place, away from the light.

SHOES

*Shoes are an accessory
that are also a necessity.*
You wear them every day, so they're
worth investing in. It's important to
choose shoes you love that also feel
comfortable, so you can walk in them.

When choosing a heel, the most important thing is that you can walk in them. There are two things to understand when considering any shoe: the pitch and the vamp.

The **pitch** is the incline. The higher and sharper the incline of a shoe, the more pressure it puts on the ball of your foot and the harder it is to walk in. People with high arches can afford to wear shoes with a longer vamp. People with low arches will have a harder time walking in very high heels. There is nothing more unattractive than a person who cannot walk in her heels.

The **vamp** is the part of the shoe that covers your foot. So a low vamp means more toe cleavage. It is sexy, sexy, sexy. A higher vamp is more comfortable and will provide more coverage and support. If you have bunions, a high vamp is best for you.

If you choose a shoe with a high pitch and a low vamp, you are basically walking on thin air. I like to find styles that have a sense of balance to them. Try to walk in a variety of different heels to see what works for you.

~ all about stilletos

PERFECT SHOES

PUMPS

You can wear a classic pump with everything from jeans to your favorite party dress, leather leggings, a skirt ... absolutely anything goes! A pump instantly gives you that elevated look and makes you feel pulled together (even when you're not).

Look for a pump with a pointed toe. It elongates the leg by creating a nice, clean line. With pointed shoes, the toe box is a bit narrower, so be sure to choose a style that doesn't make your toes feel cramped.

The top two materials are suede, which can transition from day to night, and leather, which should be reserved for daytime only. For evening, you could also opt for a pump in satin or patent.

There are also novelty fabrics; I especially love velvet and metallic leathers. As with handbags (see page 100), there are skins, pony hair, and glitter, but these are less for everyday wear. Glitter is like pony hair; once it's gone, it's gone. It can also be uncomfortable and prone to causing blisters. Your foot needs to move and bend with the fabric of the shoe, so when in doubt, go simple!

FLATS

Flats are my favorite shoes. They're the polished alternative to a sneaker. Flats come in many styles for everyday wear — ballet toe, pointy toe, loafer — and you can even find evening versions. The downside of flats is that they offer zero support, and with a softer sole, you can wear through them pretty quickly. For longevity, I recommend having them resoled regularly. Flats are a safe area to experiment, as flats go with anything and are hard to get wrong. The flat is truly your friend! If you want to get the most use out of them, avoid styles with hardware, skins, or other unnecessary details that wear easily.

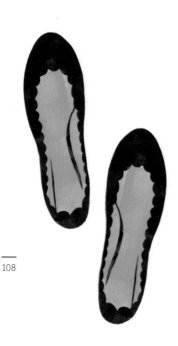

Ballet flats are generally rounder with a little bow above the toe box. They're a classic, and they go with everything.

Lace-up flats like oxfords and brogues are very versatile and can be worn with dresses, trousers, and jeans. Stick to leather or suede, or venture into patent if you're feeling playful.

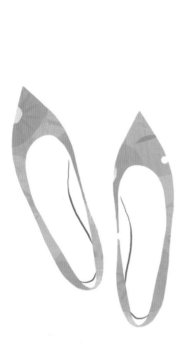

Pointy-toe flats are a stylish accent, perfect for work and running around town. As with pointy-toe pumps, they help create the illusion of a longer line.

Loafers are a preppier style. They look best with pants or with menswear-inspired looks, though you can also wear them with shorter dresses.

Smoking slippers come in a variety of materials, like velvet, suede, needlepoint, and embellished. They look great with jeans and pants and can add a lot of fun and personality to your look.

BOOTS

The **bootie** is a staple. First, choose whether you want to go for a flat or heeled bootie. Then, it's all about where the bootie hits your ankle. Pick a style that hits at the narrowest part. For most people, this means your bootie should hit either right above or right below the bone of your ankle. Showing a bit of the anklebone is subtly sexy and helps keep the look flattering.

Once you've found the right bootie, you can wear it with tights, jeans, pants, and leather leggings. As long as you pair them with skinny bottoms, a dress, or a skirt they're incredibly versatile.

The rule with the **boot** is similar to booties; here, you want to hit either just above or just below the knee. There should be no in-between. No matter what, you never want a boot to hit at mid-calf. Whether above or below the knee, boots should be worn with skinny pants. In general, pairing them with dresses or skirts is all about proportion. Over-the-knee boots look particularly good with short dresses, while longer dresses work better with a shorter boot. **Cowboy boots** go in and out of trend, but either way they can be extremely challenging to pull off. Generally, these are best reserved for cowboys, Western enthusiasts, and full-fledged fashionistas.

SNEAKERS

Ah, the sneaker. The most comfortable and questionably stylish shoe. A proper trainer is meant for the gym. A more fashionable sneaker in wearable materials, such as leather or suede, can be acceptable for everyday. There are slip-ons and lace-ups, but no matter the package, at the end of the day, a sneaker is a sneaker. Adding it to any outfit will always dress it down.

Wearing a sneaker with a dress is only advisable when done so intentionally. For example, you can pair a classic style, like Converse, with a flirty relaxed look, such as a sundress.

My rule for not screwing up sneakers is this: Keep it simple. Unless you're going to go all out and buy a bejeweled statement sneaker, simple is best. I tend to shy away from crazy colors and prints or anything too trendy. The one exception is metallic leather, which I consider a neutral.

A **shoe rack** is everything—it keeps your shoes organized and neat and helps them hold their shape. Shoe racks are especially good for storing heels. If your heels are chunky, you can actually flip your shoes around on the rack, so the front part of the shoe faces the back. I like to organize first by color and then by style.

For ballet flats and boots, I love **shoe trees** and **boot trees**. They're inexpensive and help your shoes hold their shape.

When traveling, always keep shoes in **dust bags**, so dirt from the soles doesn't spread and soil your clothes.

For longevity, I'm a huge believer in **weatherproofing** your shoes. Just be careful not to get weatherproofing spray on the soles. This can make them super slippery and hazardous to walk in.

Shoes should be stored in a cool, dry place, away from direct sunlight.

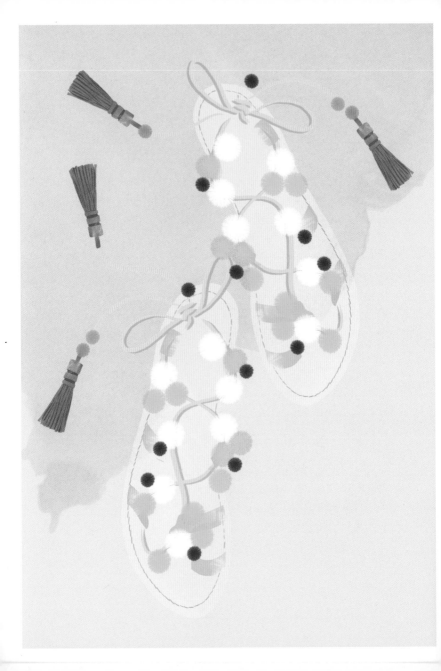

SANDALS

For something to be considered an **evening sandal**, it must have a high, slim heel. A chunky or platform heel could still skew formal, but traditionally, a true evening sandal is a more delicate shoe. As the name suggests, they are reserved for nighttime and come in a variety of materials, such as satin, suede, and leather.

Here's what you need to know about the **summer sandal**: It's an open-toed shoe that is generally playful and light. It is not a flip-flop, though it can be a slide. Fit is important here. You don't want any part of your foot to be hanging off, just as you don't want to have any extra room anywhere. If you're going to wear this style, you must always have pedicured feet. Summer sandals can be worn with anything seasonally appropriate.

FEET FIRST

Wear a Statement Shoe

As with any other statement piece, wearing a statement shoe—whether it's in an unusual color, has a wacky heel, or includes crazy embellishments—draws attention. So the rest of your look should be built around your shoe as the focal point.

Let the shoe speak for itself. Choose an outfit that is related to and harmonizes with your shoes. This could mean the rest of your look is quite simple and understated. You might opt to wear all black or maybe you choose a fun bag that complements your shoe but doesn't draw any attention away.

ALL-WEATHER

The **all-weather shoe** is generally made of water-resistant materials such as rubber or treated leather. This practical shoe exists for one reason and one reason alone: to protect your feet. However, you don't have to sacrifice style when it comes to your outerwear. Look for a dark color, a sole with traction, and a sturdy heel, plus shearling or flannel lining for cold weather. The less bulky they are, the more attractive they will be. Still, no matter how cute your all-weather shoe, you should always change your shoes when you get to your destination.

These are the must-have styles that will take you through all occasions. But once you've covered the basics, explore whatever other styles you like! Here are some to consider...

Peep-toes are shoes with a little opening in the front, and it's important to find the right size peep for your toe. Unless you have pedicured toes, go for a smaller hole. Forgo wearing tights with these, as the point of a peep-toe is to give a subtle peek of skin. The peep-toe is traditionally an evening-only shoe, as a more comfortable and supportive alternative to the evening sandal.

The **platform** can be worn by just about anybody. They are great for adding height and elongating the leg, especially when paired with a wide-leg pant. The biggest consideration when choosing a platform is the proportion between the width of the heel and the height of the platform. If you have a big chunky sole under the front base of the shoe, don't opt for a spiky or stiletto heel. Ideally, you want a heel with a little more width, to keep it balanced.

Platform sandals are great for evening, especially in classic, elegant materials such as velvet, satin, and metallic leather. Otherwise, a good rule of thumb is that a platform is either a party shoe or a summer shoe. A chunky platform feels inherently '70s. I like to keep this in mind when styling a platform and use it as a reference point for creating the rest of the outfit.

A cousin of the platform, the **wedge** is a shoe with no break between the footpad and the heel—the sole is one solid piece of material. Wedges come in a variety of shapes and heights. Wedges are more supportive and easier to walk in than heels but still give you height. The wider the wedge, the more comfortable they will be to walk in. Wedges are typically summer shoes (unless made of a winter fabric, such as velvet). You can have fun with them and style them with just about anything.

The **espadrille** is one of the prettiest shoes you can wear in the summer. With a wedge sole made of plaited fiber, a canvas upper that is easy to clean, and a feminine ankle strap, espadrilles look great with dresses or shorts and can be dressed up or down. When it comes to espadrilles, my favorite brand is Castañer, a Spanish company that has been making espadrilles since 1776! They're also the company commissioned to produce espadrilles for the likes of Yves Saint Laurent and Louis Vuitton.

Mules are shoes without a back. Though they typically have a low heel, they are not easy to walk in. To keep the look modern, find a mule with a chunky heel and some kind of a modern twist in shape or color. **Clogs** are also considered mules, as are **backless loafers**. Mules look good with cropped jeans or pants and can be filed under advanced accessorizing.

The **kitten heel** is a shoe with a low, small heel. This may bring to mind visions of a grandma, but they *can* look cool. The trick is juxtaposing them with something edgier, masculine, or unexpected on top. For example, you might pair them with distressed denim or a leather jacket to balance out the femininity. Avoid going too literal and wearing them with something vintage in feel, like a floral dress.

MATCHY MATCHY

Match Your Shoe to Your Bag

I love a matching moment. Matching your shoes to your bag is a very old-school concept, but my modern interpretation is to follow these guidelines. For special occasions, you can match your shoes and bag exactly and can even have them dyed to match. However, unless you have the exact right shade of both shoes and bag, you should create an obvious distinction between the two.

Legs for Days

The easiest way to elongate your leg is to avoid ankle straps. This creates the illusion of one single, uninterrupted line. For the longest-looking leg, wear nude shoes. Many brands now offer an extensive range of color options to match various skin tones. A nude shoe should almost disappear, which creates the illusion of a long, long leg.

You can also opt for a monochromatic look, wearing a shoe in the same color as the rest of your outfit, for a similar effect.

COLOR COORDINATING

There are two methods when considering the color of accessories:

Pull out a color If something has a print, use that as a theme to tie the whole outfit together. Let's say you're wearing a printed pump with a blue floral detail. You could carry a clutch in the same shade of blue and wear costume jewelry featuring the same color, or another color from the print of the shoe.

Practice color blocking Here, you combine multiple super-saturated hues to create one cohesive, multicolored look. Three colors is a good place to start. You can practice color blocking with contrasting colors or keep it monochromatic, with different shades of the same hue. So you might wear a solid navy top, blue jeans, and accessories in another shade of blue.

PATTERN MIXING

Pattern mixing is advanced accessorizing and takes an expert eye to style. A foolproof trick is to mix a larger print in your clothing with a smaller, finer print in your accessories. Repeating prints are easier to work with than abstract patterns.

METALLICS

When wearing a metallic shoe or bag, try to keep everything in the same family, whether gold or silver.

MATERIALS

Consider whether the materials feel complementary. Keep the dressiness of a fabric in mind, as well as the occasion. For example, you wouldn't wear a casual leather bag with shoes in a glittery mesh fabric. Generally, consider leather and suede as one category, and novelty materials as another.

MAKEUP

Makeup as an accessory?
Yes. Makeup is the finishing
touch to any ensemble,

and as such, it has the power to totally

transform a look. Before you decide on

your makeup, consider the overall color

palette of your look and the mood or vibe

you're going for. Also think about where

you are going. Getting dressed is all about

the occasion, and your makeup should

follow suit.

Rule of thumb: You must make a choice. Do you accentuate
the eye or the lip? You can do one or the other, but you
should not do both.

EYES AND LIPS

A **statement lip** can be everything. Adding a punch of color on your lips can brighten up your whole face or lend a neutral ensemble a dose of instant drama. A statement lip is an accessory in and of itself.

If you'd rather play up the eyes, you can either go for a **smoky eye** or a **cat-eye**. A smoky eye, with softly smudged shadow that extends from the lash line all the way to the crease, is more of a sultry, nighttime look. The traditional smoky eye is black, brown, or gray, but you can also experiment with colored versions. A cat-eye, with winged eyeliner that extends beyond the eyelid, creates a dramatic silhouette. Worn as far back as ancient Egypt, this look has a strong '50s–'60s vibe, bringing to mind Brigitte Bardot and her iconic winged liner. For a playful take, try colored liners in an accent color you have drawn from the rest of your look.

Although you should place the focus on one or the other, there are ways to bring out both your eyes and your lips at the same time. For example, you might want to wear both a bold lipstick and a thin sweep of eyeliner. Just keep in mind that it's all about balance.

NAIL POLISH

When it comes to **nails**, having well-manicured hands is extremely important. Think about it: The first thing you do when you meet anyone is to shake his or her hand. Having manicured hands goes even beyond style into etiquette.

You can express yourself through nail color, and these days, anything goes. Nude is a no-brainer and always the safest choice. It goes with any outfit and has the added bonus of making your fingers appear longer. Red is flirty and punchy and is a classic option. If you have redness in your skin, red nail polish has the magic ability to minimize the appearance of it. Then, of course, there are blues and greens and grays and all the colors of the rainbow. Even glitter and nail art are on-trend.

When it comes to nail polish, the only rule is this: If your polish chips, it's time to remove or repaint it!

ACKNOWLEDGMENTS

Thank you so much to Caroline Donofrio for walking me through the book process and for helping me express myself.

Thanks to my editor, Amanda Englander, for believing in this book. Thank you for our conversations, your quick replies, and your editorial insights. Many thanks to the entire Clarkson Potter team, especially Danielle Deschenes, Natasha Martin, Terry Deal, and Kevin Garcia. Margaret Riley-King, I am so grateful to you for reaching out and helping me create this book. I'm excited about everything we can do together.

Annabel Tollman, my mentor, my teacher, my role model, my best friend. Thank you for everything, I miss you every day but know how proud you would be.

Babeth, your illustrations spoke to me the minute I saw them. They've brought the book's pages to life; thank you for your creativity.

To my family, you've supported my interest in fashion since day one. Mom and Dad, you've been my number one champions. To my sister, Olivia, you were my first styling client and muse. I will never forget changing your clothes during infancy and picking out your Friday-night party outfit in high school. I love you. Aunt Nancy, thank you for teaching me about the power of a red nail and a red lip. Aunt Carolyn and Uncle Jeff, thank you for letting me live with you after I graduated college. Because of you and because of that opportunity, I had the chance to work in fashion.

To Mac, thank you for your endless support, motivation, and epic Pinterest boards.

Hallie, thank you for the late nights, the brainstorming sessions, your creativity, and for believing in me and collaborating with me.

Gail Sabella, I am so fortunate to have met you. You saw something in me and encouraged me to follow my passion.

To ALL of my clients, thank you for being my creative collaborators. I have learned so much from my work and time with you. I am so grateful for your trust and your belief in what I do.

Thanks to my agents at the Wall Group for your continued support, especially Amy and Bryan.

Thanks also to Kerry Smith, Lori and Jean, Kristi and Linda, Ed Bohlke, Ben Archer, and Jordan Long.

Last but certainly not least, thank you so much to my entire team, past and present. Without you, none of this would be possible. I am thankful for your creative ideas and input, your unique points of view, and your constant inspiration. I am so fortunate to call you collaborators and friends.

127

All rights reserved.
Published in the United States by Clarkson Potter/Publishers,
an imprint of the Crown Publishing Group, a division of
Penguin Random House LLC, New York.
crownpublishing.com
clarksonpotter.com

CLARKSON POTTER is a trademark and POTTER with colophon
is a registered trademark of Penguin Random House LLC.

Library of Congress Cataloging-in-Publication Data
Title: How to accessorize : a perfect finish to every outfit / Micaela
  Erlanger.
Description: New York : Clarkson Potter/Publishers, [2018]
Identifiers: LCCN 2017024635| ISBN 9781524761141 (hardcover) |
ISBN 9781524761158 (ebook)
Subjects: LCSH: Dress accessories.
Classification: LCC TT649.8 .E75 2018 | DDC 646.4—dc23
LC record available at https://lccn.loc.gov/2017024635

ISBN 978-1-5247-6114-1
Ebook 978-1-5247-6115-8

Printed in China

Book and cover design by Danielle Deschenes
Illustrations by Babeth Lafon/Illustration Division

10 9 8 7 6 5 4 3 2 1

First Edition